a year in the life of borrowdale bill birkett

FRANCES LINCOLN

a year in the life of borrowdale bill birkett

Many thanks
To my family – Sue my wife, Rowan my daughter, William my son –
for great days in Borrowdale. Dave Birkett for his knowledge of fell life
and crags. All the very many climbers and companions I've shared
days on the hills with. For climbing with me and being photographed:
Mark Greenbank, Steve Hubbard and Paul (Corney) Cornforth. To the
locals of Borrowdale, particularly Victor (pictured sheep-shearing),
Anne and Christine Brownlee of Stonethwaite Farm, Mr Jackson of
Nook Farm (for allowing me to photograph his gathered Herdwicks
and farm), Peter Edmondson of Seathwaite Farm, Colin Downer (for
fell, crag and climbing knowledge), Martin Weir and his staff from
High Lodore Café and Farm, Riverside Café at Grange. The current
residents of Coombe Cottage. The hardy fell-runners on Esk Hause and
Scafell (how do they do that?). John Birkett for local folklore and his
personal knowledge of fell-running and the Bob Graham Round. The
Scafell Hotel for allowing me to photograph on their property. To Peter
Hadkins and Brian Martland of the Keswick Lecture Society. To Jackson
and Anne Corrie for information about Millican Dalton and to M. D.
Entwistle for his book on the subject. To my mates in the SOGs (Sad
Old Gits): Mark Squires and George Sharpe. To John Nicoll and Kate
Cave of Frances Lincoln for having faith enough to publish this book.
To Jane Havell for producing a fine blend of the material. To those
protective bodies and groups who care about Borrowdale and seek
to protect its unique character and beauty: the National Trust, the
National Park Authority, the Countryside Commission, English Heritage
and the Friends of the Lake District.

Bill Birkett Photo Library
Bill Birkett has an extensive photographic library covering all of
Britain's mountains and wild places including one of the most
comprehensive collections of photographs of the English Lake District.
For photographic commissions, information, prints or library images
telephone 015394 37420, mobile 07789 304 949, or
e-mail bill.birkett1@btopenworld.com

*TITLE PAGE: Alpen glow lingering on the snowy heights of Skiddaw,
reflected by the mirror-like surface of Derwent Water.*

Frances Lincoln Limited
4 Torriano Mews
Torriano Avenue
London NW5 2RZ

A Year in the Life of Borrowdale
Copyright © 2005 Frances Lincoln Limited

Text and photographs copyright © 2005 Bill Birkett
Map on page 6 by Martin Bagness
Edited and designed by Jane Havell Associates

First Frances Lincoln edition 2005

Bill Birkett has asserted his moral right to be identified as Author of this
Work in accordance with the Copyright, Designs and Patents Act 1988

British Library cataloguing-in-publication data
A catalogue record for this book is available from the British Library

ISBN 0-7112-2550-8

Printed in Singapore

contents

borrowdale introduction

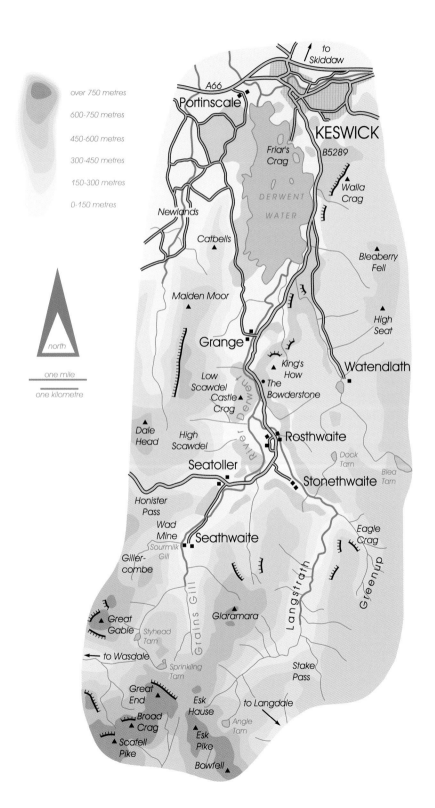

over 750 metres

600-750 metres

450-600 metres

300-450 metres

150-300 metres

0-150 metres

north

one mile

one kilometre

In Langdale, my native valley, we have a tale about the good folk of Borrowdale. In times past, they built a stone wall to keep the gowks (spring cuckoos) from leaving the dale, so we know them as the Borrowdale 'gowks'. This story makes us Langdale folk feel a little superior. It eases our hurt pride should anyone be so inconsiderate as to suggest that Borrowdale is actually the most beautiful dale in the whole of the Lake District, or mention that it has a proper lake bejewelled with islands, that its sylvan splendour is incomparable, that the soft silhouette of Catbells set against the falling sun is one of the most sublime, that its secretive offshoots, quiet nooks and crannies, cascading waterfalls and rugged steeps offer an unparalleled sense of freedom and adventure.

Even as a Langdalian I have to admit that Borrowdale, stretching some eighteen kilometres between the top of Great End and the portals of Keswick, is one of the most special places on earth. My difficulty in presenting this seasonal essay is in deciding just where to start and end. There is just so much to the valley – its many different offshoots, stone hamlets, guardian fells, mountain passes, crags, tarns, tumbling water-falls, becks and lake. So much history, folklore, characters, secret places and natural wonder means it isn't easy to define a logical beginning or a satisfying end.

Like the famous yew trees found in Seathwaite, Borrowdale has many branches. To give a simple guide to its topography, imagine it beginning on Keswick's doorstep at the downstream end of Derwent Water and proceeding southwards up the lake and on to pass Grange. Beyond the hamlet it squeezes between the rocky tree-clad narrows known as the 'Jaws of Borrowdale' to open again and broaden before reaching the village of Rosthwaite. At this point, although the general direction is still southward, it can be thought to bifurcate – east through Stonethwaite into deserted Langstrath, west to Seatoller and then Seathwaite.

The name of Borrowdale, as with so many place names in this region, comes from Old Norse: *borgar* meant a fortified place and *dalr* a dale. The fort is that atop Castle Crag, where Iron Age earthworks are still visible, a natural rocky bastion that stands defiantly mid valley in the 'Jaws of Borrowdale'. Up the valley, the hamlet of Seatoller lies at the foot of Honister Pass before the west fork of the valley leads through Seathwaite. The many 'thwaites' in Borrowdale names come directly from the Old Norse for clearing, a word used to describe land cleared both of trees and, as in Stonethwaite, rocks. The 'Sea' part of both these names probably comes from the Old Norse *saer*, meaning lake or tarn, and the evidence of the artificially straight beck and drainage channels in the fields is that once a tarn did occupy the valley bottom here. 'Toller' is thought to equate with *talar*, from the Celtic for headland or promontory, which matches the lie of the land and makes Seatoller, at the foot of the road rising over Honister Pass, the nominal head of the valley.

Here are high mountains, open quiet spaces, precipitous crags, great boulders, sylvan slopes that become a thousand shades of green in summer and a blaze of red, yellow and brown in autumn, and water that stretches both vertically and horizontally. Geology and mineralisation have produced fine green slates, gold, silver, copper and pure graphite so valuable that it was once protected by armed guards under an Act of Parliament of 1752. Stone axes were made on Glaramara by Neolithic man, people of the Bronze Age worshipped at the nearby stone circle of Castlerigg, and those of the Iron Age built defensive ramparts around the top of Castle Crag.

Later, the raiding Vikings stayed. St Herbert built his monastery on the eponymous island in the middle of Derwent Water. Poets, artists and tourists flocked to the mighty Bowderstone and the tumbling Lodore Falls. Millican Dalton, 'professor of adventure', lived in the caves and sailed his raft for over forty years. Many legends of the fell-running world based themselves here, and climbers and walkers make it their mecca. It is little wonder that the residents should want keep their cuckoo – Borrowdale is just that kind of place.

The tour

The roads are busy these days, so we'll have to limit our speed and keep all four wheels firmly and sensibly on the ground – it was two wheels in the case of the once notorious motorcycle jump over the humpbacked bridge by Mountain View Cottages (the record was landing by the fifth cottage heading north!). Let's make a start at the downstream end of Derwent Water, where the huge car park at the Headlands is often full, and walk along the shore to Friar's Crag, probably the second most photographed bit of Lakeland (see below for the first). A memorial plaque to Canon Rawnsley (1851–1920) can be seen by the path on the way. A founder member of the National Trust, his early efforts were responsible for much of Borrowdale being preserved from development. Anyone who wants to protect this landscape of tree-clad shore and island, with the ever-changing light across Derwent Water and the high fells of unbelievable subtlety and beauty of form, has my support.

Driving up the main road parallel to the east shore of the lake, first we pass under the oak-bedecked heights of Castlehead, a worthy viewpoint and a simple climb. A little further, and Great Wood provides excellent access to the lake shore (there is a car park on the left). Walla Crag, supreme viewpoint at the unforgettable height of 376m/1,234ft, lies above, with the challenging rock climbs of Upper and Lower Falcon Crags beyond.

Views to the lake and over to Catbells now open to the right, before a minor road branches off left to rise to the hamlet of Watendlath. Demanding in places, it offers quintessential Borrowdale – an isolated, time-forgotten landscape wonderfully

portrayed by Hugh Walpole in the four novels that make up *The Herries Chronicle* (1929–32): *Rogue Herries, Judith Paris, The Fortress* and *Vanessa*. A narrow packhorse bridge is followed by a car park on the right. A quick walk back to Ashness Bridge reveals the sensational backdrop of Skiddaw rising beyond Derwent Water. This view, first captured by rival photographers the Abraham Brothers and Maysons of Keswick, is probably now the most photographed scene in the Lake District.

The road rises to pass a cottage on the right where the woods open and Ashness Farm and campsite stand above to the left. Soon the oak woods close in again and a roadside car park provides access to the stunning 'Surprise View' from the rim of crags over the length of Derwent Water. Boulders stand high beside the road before the woods open again and the narrow road leads directly along the high isolated valley to the enchanting hamlet of Watendlath. Parking, farmhouses, stone cottages (one with a plaque stating 'Home of Judith Paris'), packhorse bridge, tarn and teas are all available.

After returning to the main road, Barrow House Youth Hostel lies to the left before more open lakeside leads on past Lodore waterfall, barely discernible in the woods to the left. Beyond the upstream end of Derwent Water, you pass the opulent Lodore Hotel. Trees mask the delightful little buttresses of Shepherds Crag, petite but one of the most popular rock-climbing venues, followed by the Shepherds Café at High Lodore Farm, a most delightful destination for tea and scones. The little valley of Troutdale opens to the left with the high

climber's buttress of Black Crag rising majestically above the fields and trees. Field House follows and, in a short space of time, a road over the double-span stone arches of Grange bridge leads off to Grange village on the right.

At this point, to explore the western and quite different side of Borrowdale and Derwent Water, we will take this road, passing through the village, various cafés and church to gain the oak woods of Manesty gracing the upstream end of Derwent Water. The slate house of Brackenburn, by the exit from the woods, was the home of the writer Hugh Walpole from 1924 to 1941.

The view opens to range over Derwent Water once again and offer an extensive vista over Brandlehow Point, with its perfectly sited country house, over Keswick to the high mountains of Skiddaw and Blencathra beyond. Scars on the flanks of Catbells above mark the once extensive mining activity. Copper was predominant, with gold, silver, lead, zinc and even cobalt also found in the hills hereabouts. The mines blossomed during Elizabethan times when many of the oak woods were felled to fuel numerous smelters around Keswick. Ignoring the left forks into the Newlands Valley, follow a steep drop down Skelgill Bank at the northern end of Catbells, through further woods under Swinside to Portinscale. From here it is necessary to join the main A66 road for a little way to make the return to Keswick.

However, if from Grange we continue up the main Borrowdale road, heading south directly into the 'Jaws of Borrowdale',

ABOVE: Autumnal colours develop on Isthmus Point beyond the wooden clinker-built motor launch which rests at the jetty at the Keswick end of Derwent Water. The elegant peak in the background is Grisedale Pike. The bustle of the town is only a few hundred metres away.

OPPOSITE: The setting sun hangs heavy above the western shores of Derwent Water, as a char fisherman plies his craft.

we enter what some describe as the 'real' Borrowdale. The 'Jaws' take the form of a steep-sided narrow ravine, clad with oaks and mixed woods, through the heights of King's How to the east and Castle Crag to the west. These narrows are formed from green slate: geologically harder than the rest of the dale, the rock has better resisted the awesome forces of glaciation that originally created the U-shaped valley. Particularly through this portion of the dale, the deep pools and crystal clear waters of the River Derwent take on a striking green hue – the colour of the polished slates that form the rocky river bed.

Unseen above the road to the east, beside the original, now abandoned, track through the dale, stands the famous Bowderstone, a Victorian favourite: a spectacularly large boulder approaching 10 metres in height. Wooden steps lead to its highly polished summit; the white marks on its overhanging flanks have been made by rock climbers dabbing chalk on their hands to help their grip. From the rocky outcrop and standing stone behind the Bowderstone there are impressive views to the impenetrable steeps of Castle Crag. There the hermit, adven-turer, guide, pioneer climber, pacifist, free-thinker and pre-hippy hippy, Millican Dalton, lived in his 'Cave Hotel' for some forty years until his death in 1947. In any society there are a handful of free-thinkers and philosophers – very few have the courage or conviction to turn dream into reality. In beautiful Borrowdale, Millican Dalton did just that.

Beyond the 'Jaws', the vale widens again and lush green fields, filled with contented Herdwick sheep, lead to the hamlet of Rosthwaite. The name (Old Norse, of course) means a clearing by the mound. Nearby Johnny Wood, a Site of Special Scientific Interest, is one of the richest and most unspoilt loca-tions for plant life in the region. And on the third Sunday in September every year, Rosthwaite hosts the Borrowdale Shep-herds' Meet and Show. Fell-racing, sheepdog trials, hound-trailing and craft displays are part of the agenda. Rosthwaite has a farm café, village shop, the Scafell Hotel, the Royal Oak and a variety of accommodation.

As already indicated, this is the point where Borrowdale effectively splits into two forks: Stonethwaite and Langstrath to

ABOVE: The main islands of Derwent Water, looking north-east over the bays of Derwent, Kitchen and Otterbield. The mountain over Keswick, top left, is Blencathra. One missing island, not marked on any map but known to the children of Keswick, is the 'magic' island. It exists only in late summer and early autumn, when weed parts company with the lake bed and rises to the surface to form a great raft of floating vegetation.

OPPOSITE: A red telephone kiosk, with its accompanying village sign, catches the eye in Grange.

BELOW LEFT: Against a backdrop
of Borrowdale and Derwent
Water, a lone foxhound sits
on Esk Hause contemplating
an uncertain future. Recent
legislation in the UK has
banned hunting with dogs.
My grandfather, Tommy Birkett,
wrote some sentimental songs
about the joys of foxhunting –
maybe some day they will ban
the songs too!

BELOW: An RAF helicopter and
crew practise over Esk Hause. In
emergencies they back up the
Keswick Mountain Rescue Team,
whose forty-seven members – all
unpaid volunteers – are available
24/7, 365 days a year, to assist
those lost or in distress on the
high fells. A registered charity, the
enterprise relies entirely on public
donations; it deals with seventy
to eighty incidents a year.

the east, Seatoller and Seathwaite to the west. Each fork sub-divides and branches many times as the valleys rise to the hills. Between the two, the Borrowdale Fells lead to the evocatively named Glaramara. Beyond Rosthwaite, a road leads left to the hamlet of Stonethwaite while the main road leads on past Mountain View Cottages to Seatoller. Just before the houses of Seatoller, a branch left leads up Seathwaite to Seathwaite Farm – one of the most popular starting points for those heading to the high hills beyond. Immediately after Seatoller, the road rises over Honister Pass to leave Borrowdale and descend into Buttermere.

Journeys on foot from Seathwaite and Stonethwaite, whose rainfall records claim it to be the wettest place in England, show the myriad other faces of Borrowdale. A multitude of high mountain passes lead to the valleys of Wythburn, Langdale, Eskdale, Wasdale and Ennerdale. Three of the great Lakeland mountains stand at their heads: Esk Pike, Great End and, the most loved, Great Gable (or Gurt Gavel, as it's called locally). Some of the most tranquil mountain tarns are here: Angle Tarn,

Styhead Tarn and little Sprinkling Tarn which, at 598m/1,962ft, is the highest of them all.

From high mountains to the flat expanse of Derwent Water, framed by the heights of Skiddaw beyond, from silent rugged steeps to the bustle of Keswick, through deserted open spaces to sylvan splendour, there is beauty here so intense it takes your breath away, so much to discover and enjoy that a lifetime would seem inadequate. Given this rather severe restriction, I hope this photographic essay goes some way to help your appreciation.

dwelling places

BELOW: Looking from Catbells into the Newlands Valley and over the hamlet of Little Town – the home of Beatrix Potter's Lucie and Mrs Tiggywinkle. The secret cave that Mrs Tiggywinkle lived in does exist, in the form of one of many ancient copper mines. Some of these pass right through Catbells from Borrowdale into Newlands. They are among the most ancient mines in the district and are known as 'Coffin Levels' because of their shape. They were hand-driven through solid rock ('blackpowder' explosive did not arrive in the region until the 1600s) and to minimise the work they were shaped coffin-like, just big enough for a person walking reasonably upright to squeeze through.

TOP: 'Cave Hotel' was Millican Dalton's summer refuge beneath Castle Crag for some forty years. It is still frequently used as a temporary camp by admirers of his outdoor philosophy. The National Trust seems to turn a blind eye to occasional use, although it has placed a sign above the 'Attic' (the upper living quarters) entrance asking people not to light fires or collect wood.

ABOVE: Judith Paris was the eponymous fictional heroine of the second novel in Hugh Walpole's Herries Chronicle, so this is her home only in the imagination. This cottage is just below the car park in the hamlet of Watendlath. Nestling among the hills, high above everything else, with its little tarn and stone farms and cottages, this is quintessential Borrowdale.

TOP: The slate house of Brackenburn was the home of Hugh Walpole from 1924 to 1941. In this 'little paradise on Catbells' he wrote The Herries Chronicle, a series of four novels set in Borrowdale, which contain wonderfully descriptive passages, particularly of Derwent Water and Watendlath.

ABOVE: The film director Ken Russell lived and worked in Coombe Cottage, central Borrowdale, and took many scenes for his films locally. His film Mahler (1974) included locations around Derwent Water and the Castle Crag slate quarries so spectacular that many thought they were shot in the Swiss Alps.

winter

When cold, bony fingers grip the hilltops and still all movement, Great End and Great Gable become domes of blinding white. Some would say it's a purer, more beautiful world; others, smashing the ice to water their beasts and stubbing toes on iron-hard ground, may not concur. Mountaineers, late down from the heights, stumble out of the darkness to cross the cobbles and experience the sweet pungency of Seathwaite Farm. 'If there's ice on Derwent Water, Raven Crag gully will be in condition,' goes the winter climber's mantra. Some 457m/1,500ft above valley level, the gully, usually dark and wet, is transformed into a near-vertical cascade of ice above the glacial basin of the combe, cradled between Thornythwaite and Rosthwaite fells.

RIGHT: The white dome of Great Gable rises high to the left in this view looking from Glaramara over the head of Seathwaite. To its right, Green Gable falls to Base Brown with the glaciated hanging basin of Gillercombe behind. Seathwaite provides a popular access point for all these high fells.

BELOW: Two of the three tops of
Glaramara are seen here, looking
north-west from the flanks of
Allen Crags. In the shadow below
lies the head of Seathwaite and
in the distance the distinct
outline and islands of Derwent
Water with Skiddaw topped
by cloud.

ABOVE: A row of parked cars, testimony to its popularity as gateway to the fells, lines the road to slumbering Seathwaite Farm. Beyond the farm, Grains Gill rises to the fresh snow gripping the top of Allen Crags (centre). High to the right, the cliffs of Great End are obscured by Seathwaite Fell dropping into the valley.

LEFT: Mountain View Cottages stand below Seatoller and the entrance to Seathwaite. The hanging combe above is Gillercombe with Green Gable, sprinkled with snow, beyond.

ABOVE: Leaves have gone from the trees and the red bracken has faded in this scene looking over Seathwaite Farm to the flanks of Seatoller Fell. The white hill beyond is Dale Head on the other side of Honister Pass. The scars on the flanks of the hillside are from the graphite mines, which were worked continuously for four hundred years. Also known as plumbago, black lead or wad, graphite is a pure form of carbon, chemically identical to diamond, which became highly prized. Capable of withstanding exceptionally high temperatures, it was used to line the crucibles that held the molten metals cast for canon barrels. Graphite was also the foundation of the Keswick pencil industry, which continues to this day with the production of quality art pencils.

BELOW: Leading north from Catbells, red bracken flanking Skelgill Bank contrasts markedly with the white snows topping Skiddaw beyond. Careful examination along this popular ridge will reveal mining activity where seams of copper and metaliferous minerals have been extracted. So extensive were the workings here that they spread from the top of the ridge to something like 150 metres below the surface of Derwent Water.

OPPOSITE: As the shadows rapidly climbed up the side of Stonethwaite Fell, I just managed to snatch this shot of a leafless silver birch moments before it became immersed in winter darkness. Attractive throughout the seasons, the piercing white silver bark was once used to dress wounds as it was thought to be antiseptic.

BELOW: Sheep forage for food in the frozen fields around Rosthwaite. The dominant snow-sprinkled height behind Nook Farm with its rising smoke is Rosthwaite Fell. Left of the village, with its stand of larch, is a little hill known as The How, the feature that gave the village its Old Norse name, meaning clearing by the mound or cairn.

BELOW: With all the surrounding hills in gloom, a brief shaft of sunshine illuminates the rocky protuberances of Seathwaite Fell. The rocky knoll of Rosthwaite Cam is beyond, while the barren and curiously named Tarn at Leaves lies out of sight a little further along the fell.

BELOW: With the last rays of
sun raking across the valley,
temperatures around Rosthwaite
begin to plummet. This view
looks through the 'Jaws of
Borrowdale' to Rosthwaite Fell.
The distinct peak beyond is
Pike o' Stickle above Langdale.

BELOW: *A tiny tarn on Seathwaite Fell immaculately mirrors the dome of Great Gable (left), which is separated from Green Gable by the shadow-filled recess of Aaron Slack leading to Windy Gap. Seathwaite Fell lies between the two main arteries that feed the high fells from Seathwaite Farm – Styhead Pass and Grains Gill. Consequently it remains quiet and untroubled except when the Herdwicks are gathered in.*

BELOW: In the opposite direction
from that on page 28, this view
is over Sprinkling Tarn towards
Windy Gap and Great Gable.
Styhead Tarn lies unseen beyond
and below Sprinkling. Seathwaite
is down to the right and Wasdale
to the left. In the nineteenth
century, a road was planned to
take the pass between Wasdale
and Seathwaite. Thankfully, for
the sake of tranquillity, the
scheme ran out of funds and
the route was never constructed.

OPPOSITE, FAR LEFT: Crunched by the passage of many feet, this ice on Catbells still looks attractive as it catches the evening light.

OPPOSITE: The winter windstorm of 2005 reached its peak during the night between Friday 7th and Saturday 8th January. The widespread devastation was the worst in living memory; it was reported that throughout the Lake District something like a million trees were downed in the space of ten minutes. Borrowdale took its share of punishment. Not only were trees uprooted, but trunks were simply shattered and broke like matchwood, unable to resist the immense power of the wind. The timber of the larch, most favoured by miners for pit props in roof support, is noted for its suppleness and resilience to breaking – but this specimen in Great Wood has been twisted and broken to the ground.

OPPOSITE, BELOW: On Sunday 9th January, after the worst of the storm had abated, waves still crashed into the eastern shore of Derwent Water. The normal water level is many metres away from these inundated Scots pines. Fortunately, despite having their root systems bared by the force of the water and their limbs broken, they still stand magnificently resolute. Catbells looks on with some concern.

RIGHT: A view north along the length of the shore emphasises the power of the waves crashing into the pines.

OVERLEAF: Finally the storms cleared, and Derwent Water again joined the shining levels. On the edge of the silver, Derwent Isle is to the right and St Herbert's Island to the left. The fells in the foreground comprise the distinct cone of Catbells rising to Maiden Moor, beyond which Hindscarth, over the hidden Newlands Valley, is prominent.

farming life

BELOW LEFT: Future champion of the fells, a cur (Lakeland) sheepdog pup pokes its head through the barn door at Seathwaite Farm. Its master Stan Edmondson, lifetime farmer at Seathwaite, was a champion himself: he gained a brilliant win in the 1951 Fell Race at Grasmere Sports, beating the legendary Bill Teasdale by five yards. These fell races, relatively short and extremely brutal, are the Lakeland equivalent of the 100 metres. Seathwaite is now farmed by Stan's son Peter, and the working sheepdog, responding to call and whistle, is the only practical way for his Herdwick flock to be taken to and gathered from the fell.

BELOW: A calf in the yard at Nook Farm, Rosthwaite. Built in native slate with wonderful neat aesthetics and functionality, Lakeland farms have stood the test of time since at least the fifteenth century.

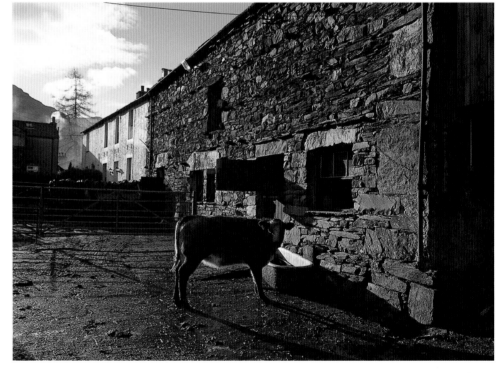

RIGHT: Stonethwaite Farm, looking out to fields, woods and sublime fells, forms part of the picturesque hamlet of Stonethwaite. Owned by the National Trust, it is a working farm run by Victor and Anne Brownlee and their daughter Christine. They supplement their farming by offering bed and breakfast: three spacious double bedrooms are available, complete with original low oak beams.

ABOVE: These Herdwicks have just been gathered off the fell and are about to be 'clipped' (sheared) at Nook Farm in Rosthwaite. Born the previous spring, they are known as 'hogs'. They are sheared for the first time of their distinctive rusty brown fleeces at around fourteen months old; they then become 'shielings' and take on the more familiar grey colour. At the next stage they will be known as 'twinters' (two winters old).

RIGHT: A freshly 'clipped' Herdwick fleece is rolled by shearer Victor Brownlee. The thick fleece has evolved to keep the animal warm and dry throughout the worst weather on the fells. Obviously a substantial source of wool, the Herdwick fleece was once of considerable value for pullovers, garments of all kinds and hard-wearing carpets. Today, it is deemed to be worthless; rather than paying to dispose of fleeces, many farmers simply burn them. What a sad waste. A kind of red paint known as 'smit' is used to mark the newly shorn sheep. Each farm has its own distinctive smit mark so the animals' owners can be easily identified. There are well over a dozen different marks (including different colours) in Borrowdale alone. Stonethwaite Farm's is two parallel red stripes on the sheep's hindquarters.

rocks, stones and posts

OPPOSITE, TOP LEFT: On the Langstrath track above Smithymire Island, great glacially ground boulders have been gathered and built one above the other to form the end of the stone wall. I wouldn't like to fall out with the person who lifted those into place.

OPPOSITE, BELOW LEFT: On the eastern flanks of Langstrath above the dub (pool) known as Blackmoss Pot stands this great boulder called Gash Rock. Climbers used to ascend the gash (crack) up its north face, so far the only route climbed to the summit.

OPPOSITE, TOP RIGHT: Found in Great Wood, this abandoned gate stoop of light green slate capped by emerald green moss and burnished with white, grey, brown and green lichens, is a work of art only nature could hone to such sublimity.

OPPOSITE, BELOW RIGHT: This finger of slate stands on the glacially polished outcrop of rock adjacent to the Bowderstone in the 'Jaws of Borrowdale'. It marks an exceptional viewpoint and clearing through the woods, over the River Derwent to the heights of Castle Crag. The horizontal scar on its side is a shot hole, dating from the 1600s or later, drilled to take gunpowder when rocks were blown up in the slate quarry.

BELOW: The Bowderstone is the biggest of all the detached boulders in the Lake District. Most books will tell you that it was deposited by a glacier, but I think it has fallen out of the crag directly above because you can see the point from which it originated. In Old Norse Bowderstein simply means balanced rock and that is exactly what it is – some 2,000 tonnes balanced on its edge. You can, and should, shake hands beneath it. It so thrilled the Victorians that they built a ladder up the side to conquer the summit in safety. It remains immensely popular with tourists, and has attracted a new generation of admirers in the form of modern rock climbers. The white marks are gymnasts' chalk (magnesium carbonate), used to enhance the climber's grip. The red object on the ground is a bouldering mat, provided to absorb some impact should a climber fall. I was one of the first to free-climb the overhanging diagonal crack (centre) – and we didn't use chalk or mats in the 1960s!

spring

Dates and times are superfluous: it is the sound of the first cuckoo that marks the start of spring. Stone walls fly up the fellsides and across the dale bottoms every which way, so why not another, perhaps a bit higher than the rest, to keep the cuckoo and this most inspirational of the seasons here for all time? There is no eagle's eyrie now on Eagle Crag, only the croak of the raven with her chicks and the scream of the peregrine protective of her eggs. Gorse and thorn blossom vie to frame the high peaks. Warmth and wellbeing seep through the 'Jaws' from lower climes and up to the heights.

RIGHT: By the shores of Derwent Water a Scots pine bough frames the snows on Skiddaw.

BELOW: Sunshine breaks through the freshly unfurling oak leaves by the side of the Borrowdale Road beyond the junction to Watendlath.

BELOW: Early spring and the leaves begin to unfold around Smithymire Island at the confluence of Langstrath Beck and Greenup Gill where they combine to form Stonethwaite Beck. The long pool, fed by a waterfall, is a favourite swimming venue during the summer months. Smithymire lies to the right and only becomes a real island when floodwater fills the man-made channel to its right. Much iron bloom and charcoal in the area provide evidence that this is an ancient site of iron production. The constructed waterway and the island's name also suggest that the waterway was used to power a forge, probably by means of a water-wheel working bellows that fed air into the furnace.

OPPOSITE: The footbridge in the central foreground crosses the River Derwent just before the river joins the lake. Over the bridge, the path leads on to pass Great Bay and enter Manesty Woods. The far woods are Brandlehow, one of the first properties purchased by the National Trust in 1902. It is hard to believe that this historic and important landmark in Lakeland history was once despoiled with abandoned mine buildings, chimneys and heaps of waste, as shown in photographs dating from around 1891.

BELOW: Resembling Medusa's head of serpents, these root mats, once buried below the ground, were exposed during the storms of January 2005. Warmer days ahead will, we hope, restore these Scots pines to health.

OPPOSITE: Two elegant silver birch trees grow from the stony scree tumbling from Shepherds Crag. This aspect looks north over Derwent Water to the white houses of Keswick, with Skiddaw rising beyond.

OPPOSITE: Rocky steps lead from Stockley Bridge, an ancient stone arch packhorse bridge above Seathwaite, to climb to Styhead Tarn and over Styhead Pass to Wasdale. One of the most used mountain access points in Borrowdale, it offers numerous options to reach the sublime heights: Esk Pike, Bowfell, the Scafells, even Pillar Mountain. The Corridor Route to Scafell Pike is one of the most famous; this was the route I first followed, aged fifteen, with two school chums all loaded with camping gear for three days and climbing equipment to tackle Scafell's main face and the formidable East Buttress. Stan Edmondson stopped us in the yard of Seathwaite Farm and asked us what we were doing. When he found out I was 'Jim Birkett's lad' (he and my father were good pals), he simply asked if we were bound for Central Buttress, then popularly regarded as the hardest rock climb in the Lakes. I said we were. He smiled and let us on our way.

BELOW: Over the head of the lake and beyond the 'Jaws of Borrowdale' stands the impressive snow-clad mountain skyline of the Scafell Massif, the highest in England. Great End comes first, to the left; then Broad Crag, followed by Scafell Pike, the highest at 978m/3,210ft.

RIGHT: Falling vertically from Styhead Beck for some 20m/ 60ft, Taylorgill Force is one of the grandest of all Lakeland's waterfalls. To reach it, go through the flat arch in Seathwaite Farm and take the bridge crossing to Sourmilk Gill before taking a path rising to the left (an alternative approach to Styhead). A little scrambling ability is required near the waterfall.

OPPOSITE, TOP LEFT: As the sap begins to rise, these red-stemmed sycamore leaves, already vibrant green, will soon unfurl from this recumbent posture to thrust out their five-pointed toothed lobes.

OPPOSITE, BOTTOM LEFT: Dark thorny shoots and brilliant white blossom reveal this to be spring blackthorn. In autumn it takes on a different guise and will be heavy with sloes.

OPPOSITE, TOP CENTRE: Thuidium tamariscinum, found growing on a rotting log in Great Wood, is a particularly attractive moss, resembling a bunch of small ferns or feathers. In Britain there are some 740 species, sub species and varieties of moss.

OPPOSITE, BOTTOM CENTRE: Fresh oak leaves absorb the sunshine by the path beneath the climber's cliff of Shepherds Crag.

OPPOSITE, TOP RIGHT: The coils of a fern unfurl among oak woods beneath Shepherds Crag. Sometimes, in the vibrant atmosphere of spring, it feels as if you can see things actually growing in front of your eyes.

OPPOSITE, BOTTOM RIGHT: Yellow gorse by Derwent Water – a common plant but very beautiful.

BELOW LEFT: Cream-white crocuses in Grange Riverside Café garden.

BELOW CENTRE: Ornamental fruit trees are popular in medium-sized gardens throughout the land. This ornamental peach, double-flowered 'Klara Meyer', is by the river in Grange Riverside Café garden.

BELOW RIGHT: Pieris growing over a wall in Grange.

OPPOSITE, TOP: Forsythia adds a splash of colour to the green slate of Grange church.

OPPOSITE, BELOW: A little lawn in front of stone cottages in Grange is the obvious place to find the famous yellow daffodil. Perhaps they were first planted by the monks of Furness Abbey, who used the village as their headquarters for the administration of the vast estates they bought in Borrowdale in 1209.

BELOW: Delightfully located above the River Derwent, this cottage is now the Grange Riverside Café.

OVERLEAF: Seen from Gillercombe Buttress, clouds boil over the end of Seatoller Fell. The fields of Seathwaite lie in darkness to the right, while Seatoller lies unseen beyond. Above the fell wall, at the point where it hits the edge falling to Seathwaite, can be seen spoil heaps from old wad (graphite) mines. Here, on the open moor, shepherds first found the gleaming grey lumps of graphite scattered among the rocks. The earliest testimony to its use is in the record books of Furness Abbey, which owned and managed much of Borrowdale: these date back to 1412 and are supposedly written in Seathwaite wad.

BELOW: On the skyline the
silhouettes are those of upper
and lower Falcon Crags, shared
by peregrines and rock climbers.
Down below, spring lambs and
their mothers share the spring
grazing with a flock of barnacle
geese.

BELOW: The western arch of Grange Bridge over the River Derwent, which runs along the east side of the village and splits into two with an elongated island in the middle. In ancient times this would have been the most convenient point to ford the river. Today, an elongated natural stone bridge spans the different legs of the river with two separate arches. It is one of the grandest such bridges in the region, being both aesthetic and functional. Both legs have deep pools which are perfect for children to paddle or swim in.

mighty trees

BELOW LEFT: Scots pines on the northern flanks of Castle Crag, near the path that ascends through the old slate workings to the summit. With their straight, tall trunks of mottled, reddish brown bark, and expansive branches with soft green needles and hanging cones, this indigenous specimen is the loveliest of all the pines. Borrowdale is blessed with a number of these fine trees, and they perfectly complement the more frequent deciduous trees.

BELOW CENTRE: Slender larches among the oaks of Great Wood, above the eastern shore of Derwent Water, frame snow-capped Skiddaw with the soft green needles of early spring. The tufts of needles, on down-sweeping branches turned up at the ends, turn golden brown and fall in autumn. The little cones resemble miniature Herdwick 'hogs' (first year lambs) in their egg shape and rustic brown colour – they played a prominent part in the make-believe farms of my childhood.

BELOW: The lemon-green leaves of autumn distinguish this lime beside the path to Friar's Crag at the Keswick end of Derwent Water. Though relatively uncommon, limes are widely distributed throughout Borrowdale, notably in Lodore Woods.

The Borrowdale Yews in Seathwaite are thought to be between 2,000 and 3,000 years old. Traditionally, in the Lake District, yews were planted next to sites of habitation; although the dwellings may have long disappeared, the yews live on to mark the spot. The first written reference to the Borrowdale Yews appeared in the 1600s; in 1803 Wordsworth penned his thoughts on them in *Poems of the Imagination*. At that time there were four together, but they suffered serious damage during the winter of 1883–84 and subsequently one disappeared. During the recent storm of January 2005 the largest yew was extensively damaged, and its highest branches severed from the hollow trunk. Most of it was flattened; time will tell if the remaining portion of trunk will recover to live on.

RIGHT: The largest of the Borrowdale Yews, with my daughter, who has climbed up the hollow trunk, poking her head out of the top!

climbing and fell-running

BELOW LEFT: Dave Birkett climbing his extremely difficult route, Bleed In Hell, taking the bold arête on Hell's Wall, Bowderstone Crag (the crag lies high in the woods above the Bowderstone). The route was so named because a crucial finger pocket was filled with quartz crystals that lacerated his finger and had to be prised off with a hammer and chisel!

BELOW CENTRE: Tumbling from the hanging glaciated corrie of Gillercombe, the waterfall of Sourmilk Gill seems particularly appropriately named when it is frozen. Here, Steve Hubbard ascends the near-vertical ice with specialist ice-axes in each hand, using the front points of his crampons driven in at foot level.

BELOW: High above Grange, on the edge of Low Scawdel Fell, Goat Crag forms a vertical face of rock. This ascent, known as Bitter Oasis, was first climbed by the legendary Pete Livesey in the mid 1970s. It was so named because a resting ledge, apparently visible from below, turned out to be an illusion; in fact there was no respite from the extremely demanding climbing. Here, Mark Greenbank is about to commence the serious moves up the final arête.

BELOW: The Borrowdale Fell Race is held annually on the first Saturday of August. Starting and ending in Rosthwaite, it climbs to Bessyboot, traverses Glaramara to Esk Hause and continues to Scafell Pike, Great Gable and Dale Head – about 27 km/ 17 miles of running and 2,133m/ 7,000ft of ascent. Local legend Billy Bland holds the record of an incredible 2 hours, 34 minutes and 38 seconds, captured on 1 August 1981.

RIGHT: On the final summit dome of Castle Crag, the climbers here are Rowan (top), Will and Susan Birkett. Climbs of all degrees of difficulty abound in Borrowdale, from the most extreme down to family scrambles. This huge diversity makes the region such an appealing venue, one of the most popular in the Lake District.

summer

Myriad white sails bob on the azure blue of Derwent Water. Oak woods, fields, clear rivers and heavily brackened fellsides provide an intensity of green experienced nowhere else. Rock pools, tumbling waterfalls, notably those in Langstrath, and high mountain tarns all help to quench the summer heat. But look and feel before you leap in the water: beneath the surface are rocks, hard places and shockingly cold depths. Some time after midnight, on midsummer's eve, strange things happen. Outside the moot hall, waiting for severe pain and punishment, a cluster of contenders for the Bob Graham Round gather to optimise the longest hours of daylight. To claim the coveted round they must run over forty-two high fells in under twenty-four hours. Beneath Shepherds Crag, taking tea, scones and cream amid the perfect setting of High Lodore Farm, rock athletes break the rules of their strict dietary regime – and love it.

OPPOSITE: Another famous viewpoint over Derwent Water is from the craggy summit of Walla Crag, perched on the eastern rim of the valley. Reached on foot in about 45 minutes from Keswick, it is well worth the effort, with an extensive panorama over the length of the lake. This aspect looks north, showing a patchwork of fields and trees above Keswick before moving on down the corridor of Bassenthwaite Lake to the Solway and, on a clear day, the distant hills of Scotland.

BELOW: By the finger of rock protruding from the northern end of Withesike Bay stands a Scots pine. The mixed woods of Brandlehow Park are a delight, and easily accessible on foot or by water to any of the landing stages on the western shore of Derwent Water.

OPPOSITE: 'A scene of matchless beauty': Wordsworth thought Derwent Water to be the most satisfying of all the lakes in the district. He described it as being proportioned in such a way as to be independent of the river and unmistakably lake-like. This commanding view looking north from King's How clearly illustrates that attribute.

LEFT: Fellside Cottage, Stonethwaite. The buildings of the Lake District are in beautiful proportion to, and blend harmoniously with, the natural landscape and surroundings. They use natural materials and building techniques developed by ingenious hands-on builders.

BELOW: Stone cottages in Stonethwaite, on the edge of the 'square' at the heart of the hamlet. Here there is just a red telephone kiosk, a post box in the wall – and very limited parking.

TOP: Perfect in function and aesthetics, Stockley Bridge – a fine old single-arch packhorse bridge made from local stone – crosses Grains Gill above Seathwaite. It has been standing securely for centuries, despite being lashed by rain and storm. Before motorised transport, it stood on the main route between Borrowdale and Wasdale that linked the heart of the Lakes with the west coast.

ABOVE: The eastern arch of Grange Bridge, with the village nestling beyond. Relatively quiet now, this area was once the centre for the richest mine in Borrrowdale, the Copperplate Mine at Ellers. 'Kupferplaten' was opened in 1567 by master miner Daniel Hechstetter from Augsburg, Germany. He and his team of German miners were imported by Queen Elizabeth I to organise and boost mineral mining in Britain, which they did with considerable success. Grange Bridge itself is a more recent structure.

TOP: Watendlath Bridge was once on the main link between Watendlath and Borrowdale – the track over Brund Fell directly from Rosthwaite, via Birkett's Leap and Puddingstone Bank.

ABOVE: This recent wooden footbridge, sensitively built by the National Trust, crosses the deep clear pools of Langstrath Beck opposite the ruined farmstead of Johnny House. It is a real boon for walkers and does not look too out of place.

BELOW: The idyllic Styhead Tarn, with Great End rising beyond. Many a hot mountaineer descending from a day on Scafell or Great Gable has taken a dip here. It is full of brown trout, and on a peaceful summer's evening it can be covered in ripple rings created by the fish jumping for flies.

BELOW: Watendlath Tarn, with the hamlet by its foot, seen from the track over Brund Fell. Again, the name derived from Old Norse says it all – 'barn by the end of the water'. The hamlet lies on what was once the main route between Borrowdale and Thirlmere to the east, over Brund Fell and Armboth Fell.

BELOW: On a summer's evening as the shadows lengthen, a lone oak stands evocatively in the open field in front of Field House. The building beyond is Derwent House, with the tree-bedecked Grange Crags above; the darkened fellside is Low Scawdel.

BELOW: From the lane near Stonethwaite Bridge, this view looks directly up the valley to Eagle Crag, with Greenup Gill rising to its left. The bracken skirting the flanks of the crag is at its greenest; later it will begin to redden. Eagle Crag stands dominant above the point where the dale of Stonethwaite splits left to rise up Greenup Gill and right into the length of deserted Langstrath. It has been a long time since the golden eagle frequented this locality, but peregrines, kestrels and ravens all nest here. Tales persist of eagles carrying off young lambs; legend even has it that long ago a baby was snatched from Stonethwaite. In vain the mother pleaded with her menfolk to try to rescue the child, so the distraught woman took on the task herself, climbed to the eagle's nest and retrieved the infant – unhurt! It is true that in the eighteenth century a long rope was kept by local farmers to enable them to descend to any eyrie in order to destroy eagle eggs.

BELOW: Quiet and little visited, Dock Tarn can be found on Watendlath Fell, feeding Willygrass Gill as it falls to Stonethwaite. It is a relatively short, though boggy, walk from the hamlet. The flowering white water lilies are at their best in early July.

BELOW: Looking over the 'Jaws of Borrowdale' and Castle Crag from King's How, slate quarries run up the hillside beyond. It is late summer: the trees remain green but the heather in the foreground has begun to fade.

OVERLEAF: A wonderful summer's evening as the sun begins to set, looking west over the Derwent Water Fells.

BELOW: The rocky head of Eagle Crag, seen from the track on the right bank of Stonethwaite Beck. The stone wall snaking up the central, lower, brackened skirt of the crag is the usual line of ascent for walkers intent on bagging the summit, although this route is by no means straightforward. Notable ascents include the classic Falconer's Crack (Bill Peascod, 1946), Post Mortem (Paul Ross, 1956) and Dead On Arrival (Pete Whillance, 1981).

BELOW: The view from Lingy End on Stonethwaite Fell. Stonethwaite Beck lies directly below, while Eagle Crag stands between Greenup to the left and the wonderful Langstrath valley to the right. The next great crag right of Eagle is Sergeant's Crag, the scene of one of Lakeland's first 'Exceptionally Difficult' climbs, made when the main gully was climbed by O. G. Jones in 1893. It was said that the initials of Jones, one of Lakeland's earliest and greatest rock climbing pioneers, stood for the 'Only Genuine'. He was pulled to his death from a precarious perch by a falling guide, on the iced ridge of the Dent Blanche in the Alps in 1899.

BELOW: The many tumbling waterfalls and deep green pools of Langstrath are marvellous places to swim during summer. This cascade can be found just upstream of Smithymire Island.

OPPOSITE: Clear green waters are the trademark of Langstrath Beck: I once caught a brown trout of some size in a dub just below this one. The farmer at Stonethwaite said it was the biggest trout he had ever seen in the beck (I believed him, anyway)!

BELOW: At the head of Greenup, above humps of glacial moraine, stands Lining Crag. The path ascending to Greenup Edge goes perilously close to the unfenced edge of the crag – anyone descending in poor visibility should be extremely cautious.

OPPOSITE: The view from the top of Lining Crag looking over the glacial drumlins and eskers and down Greenup Gill. The large shadow is cast by the dome of Eagle Crag.

wildlife

Official launches that tour Derwent Water's five landing stages, providing great access to numerous walks, are the only motorised craft allowed on the lake. Consequently, it is something of a haven for wildlife – alongside the usual residents there are many visitors seeking respite from storm and migratory flight. The extensive woods provide another tremendous and diverse habitat for plant and wildlife: Johnny Wood is one of the most unspoilt and important sites in Britain for mosses and liverworts. Butterflies and moths thrive here. The high fells are home to numerous raptors, including peregrine, kestrel and buzzard – although the golden eagle is long gone. And the red squirrel, so successful only a handful of years ago (it is Derwent Isle that features in Beatrix Potter's *Squirrel Nutkin*), has now been all but replaced by the grey.

ABOVE: One of the mute swans resident on Derwent Water all year round.

ABOVE CENTRE: This bronze-bodied iridescent green-headed duck is something of a mystery; it may be a rare vagrant blown in by a recent storm or be cross-bred with a farmyard duck.

ABOVE RIGHT: Mallards, the commonest of Lakeland ducks, swim contentedly up a little stream feeding Derwent Water.

OPPOSITE: In the meadows along the eastern shore of Derwent Water a flock of visiting barnacle geese graze alongside the spring lambs. The pile of debris, some 100 metres from the regular shoreline, marks the exceptional high water mark of the January storms of 2005.

TOP: A raven fingers the air high above the valley, its cronking croak a familiar sound among the Lakeland fells where it occupies the same mountain spaces as climbers and walkers. Stringent protection under law means that ravens are no longer threatened by egg collectors or by farmers anxious about new-born lambs.

ABOVE: Carefully lined with sheep's wool, this raven's nest has three chicks, with two eggs still to be hatched. The earliest to nest of all the Lakeland mountain birds, ravens can be with chick in March. Despite the precarious nature of their sites, often overhung and undercut on steep crag faces, their nests of twigs and small branches can reach a considerable size. The same site may be used time and again, with a new pile of twigs balanced on top of the old.

ABOVE: Eyeing its territory far below, a raven basks in the evening sunshine high on the flanks of Catbells. Despite their wild mountain existence, ravens are quite sociable creatures. They love to display to an admiring public, and often give impressive aerial shows, folding one wing and performing mid-air somersaults.

BELOW LEFT: Above the banks of the River Derwent, two red-breasted robins balance on the fence. It is unusual to see two males together, as they are very territorial – but here one bird is feeding the other, suggesting that the one on the receiving end is part of an early spring brood.

BOTTOM LEFT: This chimney sweeper, a tiny daytime moth, was rampant in mid July at the edge of a path in the open grassy area of Low Hows Wood. When freshly emerged, it is sooty black with a narrow white fringe to the front wing-tip; it becomes dark brown after a few days.

BELOW: Summer time in Great Wood, and a magnificent red admiral basks in the sunshine on the smooth trunk of an elm.

BOTTOM: By the banks of the River Derwent, this eye-catching leaf beetle (Chrysomela populi) enjoys its dinner.

autumn

Morning mists shroud the islands of Derwent Water as all the colours of the season light up the valley. The blood-red bracken runs riot on the fells; lime, silver birch, ash, larch, hazel and maple go from thin yellow to orange; chestnut, beech and oak bake to a golden red. As the gales blow, the leaves fly helter-skelter and the frosts begin to nip. Squirrels gather and store nuts and hedge-hogs snuffle into the banks of fallen leaves. It feels too good, too dynamic, and there's so much still to do – it's impossible to believe this is the end of another year.

OPPOSITE: With the leaves mainly fallen from the trees, in the foreground the autumnal reds of the bracken illuminate Jopplety How on Brund Fell to stunning effect. The view is taken from the track running from the village of Rosthwaite to New Bridge.

BELOW: The full glory of autumn is captured in this scene. In the foreground an oak stands on the bank of the River Derwent; beyond, the larch of Manesty Wood contrasts with the burnt red bracken stretching across the fellside. The path dropping from the heights is the main route off Catbells leading by Hause Gate and down above Manesty Woods.

BELOW: Above Grange and the rusty red brackens, black in the shadow, stand the crags of Nitting Haws and Blea on the edge of Maiden Moor. This hillside was once extensively mined for copper. Hollows Farm lies unseen just below.

OPPOSITE, TOP LEFT: The waxy red berries of the hawthorn are perfect for birdlife. With its prickly thicket of twisted branch and thorn, this was once the shrub of choice to define ancient trackways or delineate field boundaries – it is stockproof and reliable.

OPPOSITE, BOTTOM LEFT: The attractive Armillaria gallica, seen here on an oak root, is a familiar toadstool. It is one of the most dangerous of parasites, causing intensive white rot and ultimately death for its host; there is no cure. It should not be eaten.

OPPOSITE, TOP RIGHT: Autumnal maple leaf litter shows the variety of form and colour to be found in Borrowdale.

OPPOSITE, BOTTOM RIGHT: A dozen different leaf species float on Derwent Water.

BELOW: Below Seatoller, Glaramara House, with its interesting architecture, is complemented by a tall evergreen Leyland cyprus, standing in front of the golden oaks of Johnny Wood. Beyond are the craggy flanks of Robin Fold, topped by Robin Fold Edge.

LEFT: Fire-eaters, however spectacular, can hardly compare with the 'Jaws of Borrowdale' ablaze with autumn colour.

BELOW: Beech above the river at Grange. One of the earliest trees to colour, its autumnal grace and splendour is one of the great delights of the season. A few years ago there was a move to rid the Lake District of its beeches on the grounds that they were not an indigenous species; thankfully, the plan was defeated, and such ideas are now out of favour.

OPPOSITE: Unforgettable maple, the most gregariously coloured of them all. These trees stand by the side of the road below the Bowderstone car park.

LEFT: High in the fells, no stand of trees or even spread of bracken surrounds Styhead Tarn. and yet the colouring and season are unmistakable. Seconds before I took this photograph, this high mountain hollow, nestling between Green Gable and Seathwaite Fell, was filled with cloud – in the blink of an eye, it was gone.

BELOW LEFT: Silver birch, magnificent even without leaves, stands in front of larch heavy with needles. On the far bank of the River Derwent, the burnt gold of oaks predominates.

OPPOSITE: Bracken flanks Skelgill Bank, beneath one of the most popular mountain paths in Borrowdale. As the eye drifts off the end of the ridge, it is caught by the vast blackness of mighty Skiddaw. Ever-changing light and mood add to the heady delights of autumn. Soon the first frosts and snows will arrive, and the whole scene will be different.

OVERLEAF: Below Seathwaite Bridge, the trees and fields are still green while on the flanks of Thornythwaite Fell, running to higher and colder climes, the bracken takes on its familiar rust red. These flat meadows were once probably occupied by a tarn, which was drained by early inhabitants to create more grazing ground.

OPPOSITE: Above Seathwaite Beck, a mix of deciduous trees occupies the ground in front of a Scots pine. The beck here is confined in purpose-built masonry walls.

BELOW: A moody look into the depths of the 'Jaws of Borrowdale' from the flanks of Maiden Moor. Castle Crag, an obvious defensive site in use from at least the Iron Age, stands in the centre.

BELOW: A chestnut begins to colour in the foreground of this shot, looking from the southern flanks of Castle Crag to Rosthwaite and the upper regions of the dale. The lush green of the meadows and valley trees is still evident, while a little haze hangs around Rosthwaite Fell and Eagle Crag beyond.

BELOW: The vista north over Derwent Water from Castle Crag is simply breathtaking, with ghostly reflections off the River Derwent and the white cottages of Grange. This picture was taken from the remnants of the earthwork rim, thought to be from an Iron Age Fort, which once ringed the top of the crag. Much of it has been removed by the relatively recent (probably within the last five hundred years!) exploits of quarrymen who found this rocky knoll to be made of excellent green slate. The quarry itself was used by Ken Russell for some of the more lurid scenes in his 1974 film Mahler. If you stand on the edge be careful that you don't slip – vertical steeps lie directly below.

BELOW: Many images of Ashness Bridge grace Lakeland calendars. With the main foreground and background in shadow, and the sun illuminating the middle-ground stand of yellow-gold silver birch, this one speaks of the profundity of autumn.

BELOW: Strictly speaking, Castlerigg stone circle is not in Borrowdale but just a little above the end of the dale, strategically placed above the main lines of communication and surrounded by huge important fells. But this Bronze Age circle, the most impressive in the region, would have had a major influence on Borrowdale from earliest times. This aspect looks towards early snows on Blencathra.

OPPOSITE: Oak leaves silhouetted in silver light reflected in Derwent Water as the sun drops beyond Maiden Moor.

BELOW: The sun sinks rapidly above Derwent Water on the shore of Barrow Bay.

OPPOSITE: The delicate yellows of the weeping silver birch are, for me, the most evocative of the magical effects of autumn. Its leaves are a mere twinkle of pale yellow against the silver, and then they are gone. Beyond the lake, the cloud-filled notch marks the secretive Newlands Valley running off from Borrowdale to hide behind Catbells.

BELOW: Clouds hang over the elfin lair of Derwent Isle, the largest of the four islands on Derwent Water. In medieval times it was owned by Fountains Abbey, and on the dissolution of the monasteries it came into the King's hands in 1539. In 1569 it was sold to the German miners of the Company of Mines Royal. After several other owners, it passed to Joseph Pocklington in 1778, who built a large house on the island. Various other buildings were erected, including a Gothic 'chapel-boathouse' and a Druid circle. The 'Derwentwater Reggata' involved a mock storming of the island. Henry Marshall bought it in 1844 and employed architect Anthony Salvin to make addditons to the house. His heir David Marshall gave Derwent Isle to the National Trust in 1951; it is now let as a permanent residence, and opened to the public for five days a year.

inscriptions and memorials

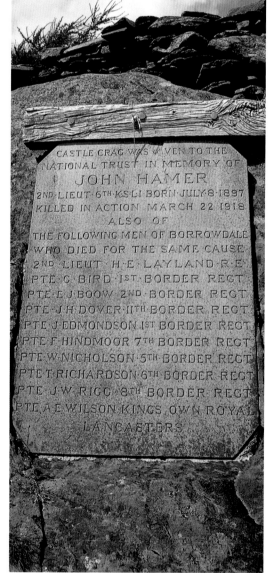

This Bridge was built
at the Expence of John
Braithwaite of Seatoller
in the Year of our Lord
1785
By Thomas Hayton and
Richard Bownefs.

I count this Folly You have done,
As You have neither Wife nor Son,
Daughter I have God give her grace
And Heaven for her Refting place.

CASTLE CRAG WAS GIVEN TO THE
NATIONAL TRUST IN MEMORY OF
JOHN HAMER
2ND LIEUT 6TH KSLI BORN JULY 8 1897
KILLED IN ACTION MARCH 22 1918
ALSO OF
THE FOLLOWING MEN OF BORROWDALE
WHO DIED FOR THE SAME CAUSE
2ND LIEUT H E LAYLAND R E
PTE G BIRD 1ST BORDER REGT
PTE E J BOOW 2ND BORDER REGT
PTE J H DOVER 11TH BORDER REGT
PTE J EDMONDSON 1ST BORDER REGT
PTE F HINDMOOR 7TH BORDER REGT
PTE W NICHOLSON 5TH BORDER REGT
PTE T RICHARDSON 6TH BORDER REGT
PTE J W RIGG 8TH BORDER REGT
PTE A E WILSON KINGS OWN ROYAL
LANCASTERS

OPPOSITE, LEFT: In Seatoller a slate headstone stands by the side of Folly Bridge behind Mountain View Cottages. Dated 1781, it reads: 'I count this Folly You have done, As You have neither Wife nor Son. Daughter I have, God give her grace and Heaven for her Resting Place.' What is that about?

OPPOSITE, CENTRE: Castle Crag was given to the National Trust, for all to enjoy, in memory of John Hamer and the lads of Borrowdale killed on 22 March 1918. That day the Germans began their spring offensive at Passchendaele. 'Up at the line again we became aware in the early morning mist of thousands of bodies, acres and acres of them, lying out on the ground, with scraps of German grey or British khaki hanging out over the stretchers' (Kingsley Martin, Father Figures, 1966, describing the German attempt to break through the Western Front).

OPPOSITE, RIGHT: Between 1913 and 1947, below the rocky bastion of Castle Crag, among the old slate workings in a cavern he dubbed 'Cave Hotel', the self-styled 'professor of adventure' Millican Dalton lived his summer months. He avoided two world wars in this manner, rafting down the river and across Derwent Water, climbing the Borrowdale Crags and Napes Needle high on Great Gable, and acting as a guide for walking, climbing and camping parties. He had a

reputation for strong opinions and was fond of debate with the many friends and visitors to his encampment. This inscription remaining on the wall, 'DON'T !! WASTE WORRDS' is thought to be the work of an inflamed Scottish friend with whom Millican had some furious arguments. Directly beneath it is written, tongue in cheek and signed MD: 'Jump to conclusions!'

RIGHT: Set in the Skiddaw slate on the steep ascent up the nose of Skelgill Bank towards Catbells, one of the finest viewpoints in the region, the Leonard plaque is often passed unnoticed. It tells of a time when the freedom of the fells – taken for granted today by the many thousands of people who roam them – was beginning to be recognised as a gift to be enjoyed by all.

RIGHT, CENTRE: This slate plaque is just below the summit of King's How, formerly known as Grange Fell. Forming the eastern steeps of the 'Jaws of Borrowdale', it offers superlative views over Rosthwaite and Derwent Water. The inscription itself is a little confusing: Louise, Princess Royal, was actually the younger sister of King George V and the eldest daughter of King Edward VII.

RIGHT, BELOW: On the side of a boulder beneath the track rising up Greenup Gill, this poignant inscription is a sobering reminder that mountains can take as well as give.

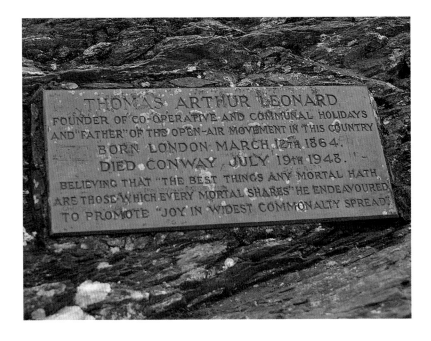

OPPOSITE, TOP AND BELOW LEFT: Not many who gaze from or across to Friar's Crag, to take in the famous and stunning view west across Derwent Water, realise that virtually beneath their feet is a rather quaint piece of local history. When a former mayor of Keswick passes on, a memorial plaque is fixed at the then water level beneath the crag. This tells us something about prevailing seasonal conditions – some plaques may be high and dry while others are now below water level.

OPPOSITE, BELOW RIGHT: Surrounded by white quartz, the Hodgson Memorial Well stands beside the Borrowdale

Road on the acute bend before the Bowderstone car park. W. Hodgson, son of a local family, was an artist of 'considerable promise' who died at an early age. Prior to motorised transport, memorial wells were a popular form of remembrance as horses had to stop and drink fresh water at regular intervals.

BELOW: The plaque at the George Hotel, near the centre of Keswick, a rich piece of history.

BELOW RIGHT: This prominent memorial to the famous critic and writer John Ruskin is on the little knoll behind Friar's Crag.

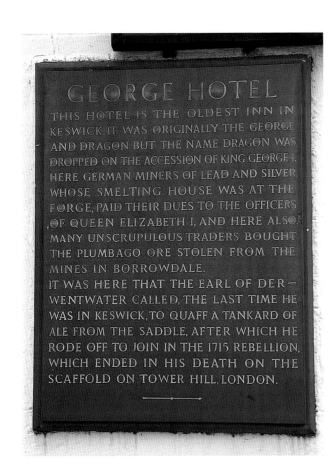

GEORGE HOTEL
THIS HOTEL IS THE OLDEST INN IN KESWICK. IT WAS ORIGINALLY THE GEORGE AND DRAGON BUT THE NAME DRAGON WAS DROPPED ON THE ACCESSION OF KING GEORGE I. HERE GERMAN MINERS OF LEAD AND SILVER, WHOSE SMELTING HOUSE WAS AT THE FORGE, PAID THEIR DUES TO THE OFFICERS OF QUEEN ELIZABETH I, AND HERE ALSO, MANY UNSCRUPULOUS TRADERS BOUGHT THE PLUMBAGO ORE STOLEN FROM THE MINES IN BORROWDALE.
IT WAS HERE THAT THE EARL OF DER—WENTWATER CALLED, THE LAST TIME HE WAS IN KESWICK, TO QUAFF A TANKARD OF ALE FROM THE SADDLE, AFTER WHICH HE RODE OFF TO JOIN IN THE 1715 REBELLION, WHICH ENDED IN HIS DEATH ON THE SCAFFOLD ON TOWER HILL, LONDON.

JOHN·RUSKIN·

·MDCCCXIX + MDCCCC·

·THE·FIRST·THING WHICH·I·REMEMBER AS·AN·EVENT·IN·LIFE WAS·BEING·TAKEN·BY MY·NURSE·TO·THE·BROW OF·FRIAR'S·CRAG·ON DERWENTWATER·

index